MARBLE SHOOT

THE HUMMINGBIRD PRESS

MARBLE SHOOT

DAVE JOHNSON

PRIVATELY PRINTED
2002

MARBLE SHOOT

Cover photograph on paperbound edition: "Boy With Stick," by
Ralph Eugene Meatyard, © Christopher Meatyard, 1995,
used courtesy of Vernon Pratt Collection and
the Ralph Eugene Meatyard Estate

Designed and set in Monotype Dante
By M & M Scriveners, Winston-Salem, N.C.

Printed in the United States of America
By Thomson Shore, Inc., Dexter, Michigan

ACKNOWLEDGMENTS

Ole' Miss Nell
can you tell
what it'll take
to make you well . . .

for
Nell Demby Johnson, 1900–1995
and
Papa John
who never forgot to hug me.

Thanks to my mother for all her encouragement and to Jane Rebecca for her endless support. Thanks also to Kurt Brungardt for listening to me read these poems over and over and for living with me in the fire and to Greg Fraser for reading my work with a hawk's eye. Thanks to Sam Peabody in the summers. Yes, your Georgia saved me.

Special thanks to Robert Hedin for giving me poetry, to Marie Rogers for turning me on to language, and to my readers: Dan Halpern, Dillon Johnston, William Matthews, and Lee Potter.

For his evocative print, which appears in the cloth bound edition, I wish to thank David Faber, a magical artist who conjures up visual poetry.

To my editor, Rosalind Tedford, thank you for all of your endless hours. And a huge thanks to Harold Tedford who believed in these poems enough to see them through to publication. And to all my people I have left out, thanks for your wishes.

CONTENTS

DOWN THERE

IN HERE

UP HERE

OUT THERE

SOMEWHERE

DOWN THERE

COMING HOME AFTER TAKING
GRANDMA TO THE DOCTOR

On the highway between Charlotte
and Jefferson, dark blacktop
over state lines
rides into sand.
To the south, the pavement—
light gray, bump after bump of stones,
diamonds.

Miss Knight, in Sunday School,
told us about streets paved
in gold, pearls, and diamonds.
This was it.

Later, in third grade, Miss Donahue showed
a map of America.
South Carolina. *This is where we are.*
It was awful small compared to the rest.
Shaped lines
outlined in red,
like the diamond on the back of the comic book-
a girl's best friend,
diamonds are forever.
The state like a diamond
state of diamonds,
diamondback rattlesnake.

BAKING ON SATURDAY MORNING
WITH MY MOTHER

My mother and I mixed batter like the old pros in the bakery shop.
She did most of it. I just helped. Six years old, my face freckled
      with flour, my hands sticky with egg yolk,
she never let me break them.

She was good at that. She could crack with one hit of the counter,
one in each hand making side jokes about the boss and my father.
      I just threw out the shells, putting my fingers
in the gummy residue on the way to the garbage bin. I got dirty too.

She would crank that electric mixer wide open. It had several speeds,
but to her there was no in-between. It was either off or racing.
      She talked to me loud but I couldn't hear a thing,
just the sound of the motor turning like my uncle's boat going fast.

The spin of those silver beaters turned everything yellow and white and yellow
till it was ready to pour in the pan. She turned on the oven light
      so I could watch it rise. I had to sit
on the kitchen table to see it. The smell lifted all over the room.

She told me, *you are the watchman*. She washed up and went on
and I stayed, my glued hands balled up, waiting for the buzzer to go off.

ELLIC CAMEL GETS A HIT

On day three forty-seven of Ellic Camel's sentence,
Miss Allie took me to see the opener at Camp Field.
Four guards lined the outfield: one behind the umpire, one by
the foul pole, one in the bird's eye, one just over the mound.

On the first base side was the Gibson drive-in, where we got
hot dogs and cotton candy for a quarter. Free colas
were given out after every home run. And just behind
the backstop Roy Jowers sold corn liquor in Ball fruit jars.

The place was packed, kids and old folks. Adults cost a dollar,
kids fifty cent. And if you wanted a spot in the shade,
under the tin roof, it was two dollars. Most time we sat
outside. Sometimes that hot silver tin would just bake your head.

That day Ellic Camel got a big hit and everyone
cheered him on. He was barreling around second, headed
for third, a standing triple, but he just kept on running,
out of the base path, by the dugout, and through the entrance.

Somebody left the gate open and Ellic just took off.
The umpire called him out, but he just kept on. And when he
was about ten yards outside the fence, the fans all sucked air,
it sounded like the whole stadium was left on one wing.

No one said anything and all the guards just watched him go.
Like a match dropped in dry woods, the fans rose up, one by one,
cheering till the whole place went up in flames. Jack "the runner"
began taking bets and almost everyone took him up.

We were glad. We forgot what he did and we did not care.

From nowhere rang a hammer. He went down wriggling, plucked
in half. His hands gripped dirt. The crowd was dead. He was dead. I
died. And Jack "the runner" jingled change in a coffee can.

CLEANING THE YARD

Every year, about this time,
Miss Allie tied brush brooms

of chicken wire and branches
of magnolia and oak.

We swept the sand yard, raking
brittle into moist rot;

yellow, red, and brown furrows
winding to piles of churned
                              aroma.

The dead combed clean.

And when we were done,
I pulled down my stocking cap
                              and dove.

CIRCUIT PREACHING

Every Sunday Daddy piled us in the car,
drove sometimes as much as three hours,
to a different stop.
We never skipped a week. Mineral Springs,
Cedar Grove, Antioch, New Hope,
Trinity, Fork Creek, Rock Creek, Clear Creek,
and Back Creek. Including the hymns,
the service rounded out to an hour
and seventeen minutes. He had it down
to a science, that every Baptist's attention span
lasted twenty-four minutes, and at the end
of the allotment, he would lead an altar call
every head bowed, every eye closed.

One Sunday he prayed loud, louder than I'd ever heard,
fierce, for someone to give in
to come down. The piano whipping pianissimo
to forte and back. Not one soul moved. He prayed
harder, his glasses steamed with forehead sweat.
No one moved. He gave a last call
for all sinners to come home.
I wanted to go. No one came.
He gave the benediction, the people lined up,
and one by one he greeted them out,
his face growing smaller with each hand.
If only one hour of Jesus on Sunday's enough,
how the hell will they ever make it through eternity?
I stood beside him, alone, nothing but hardwood, empty aisles,
and his voice swirling around the vestibule.

COOL AFTERNOON IN THE AUGUST SHADE
AT JULIAN JENKINS'S PLACE

Late yesterday we went back to thump heads.
One by one, Miss Allie would count and count back
thirty days since we first saw them.
She sometimes thumbed a whole row
till finding the ripest.
With a swift stroke
she plucked the cord clean.
Rubbing loose sand smooth, round
bottom, she placed in my hand
the one to be carried back to the cedar block.

While I waited, anxious,
weight heavy in my five-year-old hands,
she skimmed the wet rock
pulling her blade
tight.
       She raised her pale arms,
pushed off on her toes, creaking brogan leather
a dark silence of razor through thick air.
Flesh splitting green,
rind then red
veins pushing,
meat juice, blade *thud* into wood;

       the one
head
                   wobbling
          two
on their halves.

She slipped her warm steel
into the deep
heart, dashing me a piece
as I came with palms open,
up for the cool melon.
Mud water dripping from my face
down my naked chest.

DAVE GIBSON MAKES HIS WAY DOWN

Seven Sundays in a row he fell
on his knees at the altar
of Rocky Creek Presbyterian.
The twins sang *Just As I Am,*
and granddaddy Russell prayed
up the invitation,
for folks to come accept,
to rededicate and be washed clean.

And those seven Sundays, I counted them,
Dave slipped out
past his wife,
and swaggered down the aisle like a pine
in a sand storm. He swirled round,
bending, holding to his hardwood feet,
his only roots between this and that other world.
He fell hard on his caps,
his greased hair falling down
around his face, shaking his head
crying for forgiveness.
One of the deacons gave him a handkerchief
and he blew and cried and sang,
without one plea. I come. I come.

The twins wound up the seven verse song again
and Dave said he was sorry,
to his wife, his children, to the congregation.
He knew he was an awful man,
but *the devil just got into him.*

And on the eighth Saturday, Mrs. Lucy watched him
come home drunk again.
When he fell in that night, she pushed him
into the parlor and onto the oval rug.
She tucked him in like a jelly roll
and began sewing the ends up.
Dave sang and laughed, and snored.
She sewed. In an hour she had him stitched in.

She went out and got a mule whip, rearing back
thrashing him, her face red, she gritted her teeth.
And snores begat murmurs and murmurs
begat shouts, and Dave Gibson was begging,
please stop, please Lucy.
And she beat him blue. He swore he'd never
drink anymore, and she beat him.
And then he swore he'd go to church every Sunday.
And she still beat him.
He told her he'd love her forever.
She kept on.
And he said he'd repent. She beat him harder.
And he said he wanted to die.
She beat him.
And he said he'd never repent again.
She stopped.

The next day, he sat in the same pew,
eyes black, jaws blue.
The twins sang. Every one bowed to pray.
And Dave, his lips dry white, parched,
stared at the open cross behind the pulpit
and said nothing.

JUST OUTSIDE THE TOWN LIMITS

This is the way wet clay quietly holds
the sprigs in place, this Silver Queen corn
we planted each spring.
       This green wind, the lighter knot
on the edge of the wood pile,
the notes that the spruce blows back:
wallow, willow, wash, whip.
       In the old kitchen the long white deep freeze
opens and closes like a casket.
Clip. click. Clip, click.
       The front door, heavy and wooden, is held
by a dye rock.
Dye stone, dye wash,
the scrubbing of washboard all the day's work back.

CUTTING WOOD WITH MISS ALLIE

Yesterday was the last day
we would bow to pray.
We took the same path
through the blackberry
thistles, out back
beyond the row of blackjacks
to a big yellow pine.
Miss Allie took out her ax,
the one she'd sharpened
since late September.
She handed me her small sledge,
closed her eyes,
with a gasp
                    whaled into the trunk. Blow
after blow, she grunted, cold heat
weighing heavy with each breath.
She nodded and I began
pounding.
We chopped and hammered in rhythm,
chipped the fleshy pine
tar bleeding.
The silence of steel in wood,
cold ringing
every tree living.

LEAVING MOTHER AT HOME ON THANKSGIVING
TO GO FISHING AT THE OUTER BANKS

It sounds like backwater, black water, water dark
as the winter sky
lapping against the dock in the Morris Marina.

The captain stands at the restaurant doorway
with a canteen and a cup of coffee.
The mate scrubs down the deck with a heavy broom
like a large toothbrush in the mouth.
The fog is lifting.
          Every year I stand here in my sleep
with my father and his friends, holding my
fish poles, waiting
like all the others, all the rest
to get to the other side
to the ocean side,
to the really deep water, the sloughs of these Outer Banks.

Sometimes standing scared of this big water,
I think of the story in Sunday School,
a man eaten by a big fish.
And one in grade school,
a man rowing to sea and waiting for one until he died.
And my father,
the one who always got away.
I guess everybody has a fish story.

But this morning waking into mid-winter,
the harbor long since closed for the season,
more than one hundred and fifty miles away
from that hill land, dry land, sand land,
dreaming of my pole bending double,
after such a long wait in the cold,
in rain—I too know, it is just a story,
of water dripping in my mother's kitchen sink.

AFTER GRANDDADDY PREACHED FROM GENESIS

Luther Miles got drunk and told me how it really happened.

Low in the cool, dank basement of the earth,
four Gods with strong heavy hands
set out to see the sun.
They all took the same path,
but somewhere
in the dark

one stopped for water.
He saw some shad
skimmin' across the river.
They wuz be'in chased by a wood duck.
He swam up.

One heard noises, clambered up a tree.
He saw some birds, a sandpiper peckin' dead crabs
and a giant ole' buzzart circlin'
He flew up.

One, took the straight and narra',
well he jus' went up in flames.

And the other,
he got tired and sat down to take a nap.
he woke up two thousand years later,
finding he forgot the whole damn thing.

After evening service I told Margaret Anne and Regina how
it all came out. Aunt Lou heard me and she grabbed me by the
ear, took me into the church, right up to the altar and told me
to ask for forgiveness. I stammered, crying through a prayer,
as she twisted my ear. Then she took me to the wash room
and lathered my tongue with Lava and told me she ought to
tell my daddy. At supper the whole family sat around the table.
My face red, my right ear on fire, and my mouth inside out.
Daddy said the blessing and I lipped my tea and saw the gray
soapy film fill the glass. I was flush. I knew he would beat me.
I waited for Aunt Lou to say something. All night. But
she didn't. She just glared at me across the table.

Five years later she left my uncle and two daughters for a
professor at the college in Hartsville. Mama told that Lou said
she was tired of living in this backwater Baptist country. *And
for that, she'll have to answer.*

STAKING THEM OUT,
IN BECKY MACDONALD'S
OLD COW PASTURE

Two hundred and fifty Big Boys, Better Boys, Margos, Rutgers, all mixed together they grew, some to six and a half feet. My part was toting five gallon buckets of water down each row and pouring a coffee can full in each hill. Miss Allie came behind me, fell to her knees, to push the roots deep into the mud water. With her fingers—red clay flesh—she pulled them out of the ground, dragging the sand around the base. Loose grains clung to her hands like tiny planets trying to find an order. A strand of her tied up hair fell to her face. Looking at her new hands she brushed it back with her forearm. Her hair fell again. She brushed it back. And again. She finally gave in and scratched her forehead with her pointer, the muck sticking to her brow.

Standing, she picked up the two-by and hammered the pine wood stake while I held it firmly in the sand. One for each plant, she tied them up with old panty hose, the white crotch hanging down, round the stem, around the stake, lifting the budding tomatoes high. Again she pounded and I held, each stroke jarring my small arms, my chest, my stomach, and on the last strike it even tickled me down low. Intertwined, her arms like heavy high wires sagged on her breast, on my back, twisting round me. All in this mud swamp water cow dung on my feet.

NO ONE WOULD TAKE ME FISHING

for two weeks after Sam Camel fell
in old man Boatwright's cove.
They had to pull him up with a drag
tied to the front-end of Miss Allie
and Luther's pickup.
The net coiled
like a black snake, turning
his face blue with blood
and his eyes bugged out
like a crappie, a hook snagged in its lip.

IN HERE

SUNDAY COOKING

In the next room it smelled like a vat of dark collards
you could pour out lifting the whole kitchen to the next floor.
And I remember the room spinning
like a child's top shot from a plastic gun, like the plastic tray turning
one of her cakes on an early Sunday morning.

I think about the potatoes she peeled once a week,
how she cut out those eyes twisting those little oblong globes
her thumb always on the edge of the blade,
ten pounds at a time of those blind diced whites.
And in the end there was nothing left but a pail full of brown skins and bad places.

In the dream that rises back like the smoke
from this little house, my mother has smoothed
the top layer on the cake. She steps back and pulls
that long knife between thumb and fore,
the icing builds like snow caps on the tips of her fingers.

Throughout the house, even in the back room,
where I put my face in a towel that has been hung up to dry,
I see her standing back eyeing her work,
hands high in the air like a tall bird in a moment's hold waiting
as if she will just suddenly fly off.

SISTERHOOD

Letting go of all notes of sound the water rises.
It is night time. We are at the piano.
You hover over my shoulder counting your fingers.
It is a cold autumn, cold raining.

The night is nowhere grey. We get up and dance
and put our lips against the bay window,
our breath blowing fog, seemingly through the glass
beyond the evergreen.

And like calling a new name, you pull back your face
and laugh at my pushed up nose
kissing the pane.
The piano air is ringing still.

I reach to hug you deep, your back
to everything else.
The embrace I have been holding
for something far away.

Your arms wrap me, my hands lock on you,
and I listen to my body sing.

MISS ALLIE'S PARLOR LIGHT

I plunge upward for the beads,
the darkness
compressing my chest,
my ribs roping, twining me
into knots.
I cannot breathe.
My eyes wide as purgatory,
I see
nothing, endless coils,
circles on circles.
Panic waving of hands
through empty air,
I catch
no string of light.
I spin into drunkenness,
into darkness, everything is cross-eyed.

Quickly, I tighten
my eyes, lids twitching,
head bulging;
my mind sees a full fiery-moon
against the window.
A clear reflection:
left of the bulb
from a small ceiling hole,
seventeen silver beads
linked, attached to bright
red gift-wrap ribbon,
tied to a bronze palm-sized crucifix.

Reaching
just above my head,
the cross, cold
heavy against my flesh
I prick my fingers
on his thorns.
I gently pull down.
The heat burns my chest,
my eyelids click.

SITTING IN THE HOUSE

At dusk this evening I watch from the window,
the shingles waving from the roof of the barn.
I turn flat to see a mirror by the door.
It is all framed in blue.

And beyond the cloud cover,
the sky opens and the rain pours all around.
I can see far into the next county, into that other world;
          it is all wrought iron with a circular base, a bulb
hangs from a stand. The light sways, the shadow swinging
slowly and a small coal in the fireplace fizzles low.
We're all going dead.

I wanted to just plant something
more than myself. Harvest a little more.
I hear a grasshopper in the tall weeds and I see
this much earlier than I expected. Crickets and katydids
on hooks taking stringers of bluegill. Someone has caught me
to catch something. Maybe Daddy, Daddy Russell, or all
those others were right. Just one name after another.
I am one link in a long chain that might be broken.
I am the last son with the family name and the whole family knows it.

Let these gates fall away
and bones get up and dance,
a turn,
a reel into stone.
Moon, claim us while you can, soon, the sun will burn this water black.

THE LIVING ROOM

Here there is no measurement of anything,
but everything carries its own beat
like the clacking of that wooden metronome
over the piano in this dark living room.
The space we never used for anything
but the Christmas tree and long afternoon
scale practicing. Some days I would go up
and down those tainted keys and feel the weight
of the foot pedals drop over the room, the dark-faced
Indian breaking back into the house, the chime of the
ringing glass all kept in time. You used to tell of
those pickled eggs and warm franks with sweet chili relish
that let him break back into your heart.
The teetering dancing man toppling round and round
in your cold living room. He had nowhere to go.
The thief in his own home.

Years later your mother told you to take the piano.
We moved from her house to ours. The music moving
in and out of houses, in and out of bodies.
There's no where else for it to go.
Put it in the living room, you said.

I remember you sitting down and studying those keys,
with eyes that went on long past dark.
With one stroke of that creature you made demons rise,
lifting your thin lean legs off the bench,
your nimble fingers taking one key at a time,
faster and faster till the whole board turned
to one black and white blur.
You went from pulling the Entertainer to Amazing Grace
and back without even a break in the rhythm,
the whole scene in circles,
that dark Wurlitzer rising off the floor.

And this evening I'm breaking back into the house
into your heart, into his, and all of us going back
to the primal caged dances of one tribe to another.
Where does a white man go, where does a Cherokee go,
where does anybody go, knotted up not knowing who you are?
The doors are all locked, all the lights are off except an occasional lamp,
the shades are pulled
just above the windowsill
and if you listen close enough you can hear the faint sound
of the backs of sweaty legs pulling, lifting themselves off.
The player is looking under the seat
for another book. What song will be next?
What's the next story? It's another long night waiting
for the breaking of street lights, for them to give way
and go out. The only sound rising is their buzzing,
the one two shuffle of feet, and a fumbled
ring of keys until they drop dead on the dark wood porch.
The silence of the heart breaking back into the body.

LOOKING IN A MIRROR AT MISS ALLIE'S

Aunt Sara says,
you've got your mama's jaw.
Miss Allie says,
that's your daddy's nose.

In every breath,
the dead sing through our lungs.

Glancing down at my feet,
my ankle,
I am under the black walnut
in Grandma's yard,
my toes digging in pure
white sand,
culling it brown,
then black. Dark
as that light
in her bedroom,
the one I see as she lies beside me.
This ankle of hers.

MISS ALLIE'S BUTTER CHURN

I watch intently Miss Allie whirling
the round Ferris wheel,
the blue rivers
of her arms bulging,
her brow beaded with greasy exhaust.
The musical clanging of the oval,
the churning of wood
against wood,
my stomach leaps
to grab the controls:
Mother Mary, she's done!

It is time.
        I stare down
on her sun spotted skin.

Miss Allie reaches under
the smooth oak tent.
She puts the golden half-moon in the sky of her palm.
She pinches it and brushes her lip.
She glares up at the high chair,
dabs the slick milk for me.

Doggedly, I lap her finger,
her crusty thumb nail.

UP HERE

ON THE FIRST DAY

I cried hard at the loss of my body pushed down into thistles.
Scrambling up I grasped vines wrapped around birches,
briars pricking my skin pointy green and white into my knuckles.
Pulling away deep layers, I held the fists of knotted elms
in South Carolina, in Miss Allie's country, at home.

I wanted to go back but got nowhere close to the place within.
I lay below thorns, dry scabs, begging for no more.

Then I forgot my body was dead.
Like everything had been prayed back together,
you came over asking the walnuts, birches, elms
and all the dead wood to rise and leave this dark sand.

And when I came to beg the trees to stay,
the brambles swung up, back into place, leaving me down.

Now as I lay face down in this deep, rich soil,
in this sand hole filled like those in cemeteries all over the South,
the ones that slough, graves where the dead surely have left,
I am coming in myself, out of you, out of Jefferson, Carolina, the South,
out of all its great dead.

And here, the only place I can ascend, peeling back one by one,
geese flap into black buzzards.

ON THE WAY TO WORK

this morning, I remembered the day Aunt Lizzie
was put away.
Shovel after clinking shovel,
two boys threw dirt on the silver box.

All morning, I heard the rain
falling deep,
and the dead sound of the dirt
like a hand coming down hard.

MISS ALLIE'S STONE

for Miss Allie Miles 1900-1984

Every night I see her.

It's always
morning
after last night's sandstorm in Jefferson.
It's always
one hour after sunrise,
dirt road lit,
one blue bulb blur.
It's always
shadowing her two starved setters,
foam on their mouths.

Far off
sand covers the S in MILES
I reach down,
brush her clean.
Katydids rise, dancing from her stone.

MISS ALLIE READS TO ME FROM SLEEP

In summer 1972, Chesterfield County,
the moon was so big it lit up the whole yard.
You could see ten, fifteen miles down and over
the sandhills. Nothing could have been brighter.
I walked down the sand road between
the Antioch church and home, the sky clear as day,
fields clear as sand, stone. That pure white sand.
That year we plowed all day and most of the night.
It was God's year, we said, and when harvest came
we had three times the barn would hold.

The sand was cool, the moon
so bright they told stories
about seeing the dead. I never believed them.
Every night that summer, I passed Antioch
and looked for all they said they saw.
It was never there. And I often stopped
and looked real hard in hopes of seeing something alive,
but I couldn't even deceive myself.

Last night, nineteen years since,
I slept through the walk past Antioch.
And I saw them. They were all there.
And they were eating and smoking,
two of them playing cards for money.
Elmo Crowley was drinking Rock-n-Rye.
Uncle Vernon, Load, Aunt Lizzie,
they were all out there stewing pork links
on hoe cake bread. And in the corner of the yard,
Miss Allie sat reading a book. I couldn't make
it all out, but it threw me back,
to when we were all alive, and she was telling me,

look above the moon,
on the first full of summer.
Way back, in the corner
of the sky, you'll see a small stone
that lights up so big
you can see the dead.

I turned around to see it.
And when I passed the cemetery,
sure enough, they were all there.
Granddaddy was preaching to Clarence Johnson
for stealing that gas. Luther Miles was listening
to a ball game on the radio. Oddis Leer was stoking
the fire. And Miss Allie sat alone
in her gray rocker, mouth full of Navy,
and she was just reading from that little book.
Too big to be a Testament.
She looked up at me, pulled off her specs,
and folded the book in her hand.
She spit black, brown deep
into the moon,
the sandwhite, sandstone.

GRANDDADDY RUSSELL AND
THE LORD COME VISITING

After Granddaddy Russell died it wasn't long till all his folks went on. Lizzie, Load, Uncle Vernon, Luther and Kay went down like flies. And not long after that, Daddy quit his job to preach. It was mid September, just before I was to be saved for the first time. We were at evening service, when preacher Malcolm Ivey caught Daddy by the arm while we were lingering in the vestibule of New Hope Baptist Church. Reverend Ivey told him, *you should be doing something for the Lord.*

Three weeks in a row this happened. Daddy began to have lock-down spells. He couldn't breathe and started on nerve pills, but nothing helped.

On that warm Sunday night under the oak tree, in the gravel parking lot Daddy gave in. He broke down, cried in his hands. Something hard to believe, this two-hundred and ten pound, thirty-four inch waist, cannon biceps man falling to pieces. He had told us almost once a week how easy we had it. How he had plowed a hard-tail mule to get this body. And on that night he was going back into the furrow to walk that line. Mama had to drive home. He couldn't see. And we couldn't understand. He said he had something to tell us. We got home, Mama leading him to the bedroom, shutting the door behind. They didn't come out for a long time. Becca and I could hear them crying. She looked up at me and asked what was wrong with Daddy. I said nothing. I knew she'd never understand. I didn't.

Mama opened the door and blew past us. Daddy knelt by the bed, his head in the blue quilt, his knees brushing the tassels that hung from the spread. His large body quivered, moving up and down with the rhythm of his crying. Becca and I stared, daunted, scared. Mama down the hall, Daddy on the floor.

THE MONEY MARKET

Every morning my mother punches a ten key,
hour after hour the clicking and spitting of numbers.
None of her money.

Every morning my father cleans print rollers
for the money-makers in the government building.
None of his money.

It's cold. I can't move.
Everybody is up,
but all I can think of is a warm evening storm.

Water drips in a hot greased pan.
A hot greased pan.

In Carolina, everywhere, the yards are coming to life.
Linens, sheets, towels whip windlessly from hand to hand.
And the mills are churning.

Lazarus, take up your bed and walk.
My heavy footed mother rings as she runs
down the hall.

Two things we all must do:
pay taxes
and die.

She knows we're waking
into this sleep of death,
into this no money market of ours.

ONCE AND FOREVER

According to the early Southern Baptists,
the ones I knew, Daddy Russell, Preacher Ivey,
Reverend Sailor, and my father,
you only needed to be saved once.
But since that warm September evening,
at the James Robins Crusade, up in Wadesboro,
I have begged to be saved over and over.

Oh you could backslide, fall by the wayside,
but you just ask forgiveness and it was *all washed clean*,
no need for another saving.
        Once saved, always saved,
rattled off the tongue easy
like skimming stones.

Some nights I drink, sometimes just a cup of tea,
sometimes a few words from *James*.
But every night it's the same story.
I sleep with a stone, a sleeping stone we call it.
Some nights it gets cold and I lose it between the sheets.
I wake to not having it in my hand,
I fumble to find solid ground.
When its cold, I pull it in and rub it.
It gives me heat,
something to believe,
something to ease me into the dark.

SITTING IN A GREEN KITCHEN ON TWELFTH, DREAMING OF WHITE A LONG WAYS OFF

And now, here, as the figs sit stewed
in a pot that has boiled over
from time to time,
as the clock in the next room
is about to strike twelve, it has stopped;
no one has wound it,
hung at the same moment
unmoved, unshaken.
It reads the same
                    every time I pass
I see you come wandering, dreaming
down the hall
in your white gown, the one
you would have worn.
The smell of that sweet fruit
on your dress
flows into the space
like a last ditch effort
to burn the hair right out of my nostrils,
to peel back my skin,
to take back my bones sweating thick mud.
          The swamp water is rising over me.
There is no way out of this tangle
of fruit, these vines, these buds,
limbs, leaves, root flowers
twining over us, pulling us into a bed
of morning glories,
and back
to the edge of the water.

OUT THERE

MISS ALLIE'S OLD FORD

She had all intentions of coming home,
coming back to fix it—
the rusty two-ton
in the yard.
To put
all its pieces together—
the steering wheel, the gear shift,
those shiny red doors.
To put back that Jersey heifer, that sow
whose belly hung big as the moon,
those two pink runts
who never once sucked,
and me
atop that pile of steaming manure.
Not the way it is now.
Not the termites
burrowing the sideboards.
Not these ants
erecting sandy temples
under the seat.
Not these rattlers
coiled in the engine,
waiting to pray.

43

TWO WAYS HOME

The three-toned sprayed on '72 Impala
had a radio that played on and on,
AM songs that were all blue.

One shade a little lighter than the other, under the ragged leather top,
dulled the whole day
when you raced up the street
to save my life,
to save me from the bad guys,
the day the bus came home without me,
the day after two little girls were snatched
while walking home from school.

I saw the lines of fear running across your face,
the crow's feet that always fly a straight line home.

And when you cornered me in that back room
telling me I could have died,
I heard the clinging of the belt rack
saw the room go upside down,
and then the radio came back on.

      It's the middle of the night again
and we're in the car on the highway south,
coming home from seeing a great aunt.
I'm lying in the back seat, my ear in the cushion,
the tires bouncing off the turnpike.

"Ka-thump.
          Ka-thump.
                  Ka-thump."

From street light to street light
the beat eases me into the darkness,
and all I can think is how I don't want the car to stop.
Just you and me. I want to lie here forever.
I want you to just keep on driving.
I want the night to never end.

MADE IN THE SHADE

Pond of passion, the height of summer sun.

This was always like this.
The screams of June Bugs,
the wet wallow of the Bull Frog,
the young girl watching her cork slowly rock red
to white to red, the little circles moving away
get bigger and bigger.
       This alone
is the hedge of innocence, time, sitting warmer
pushing the day's heat on.
And a woman far off cries out a call
to lunch. The girl looks up.
A bird in the hackberries flips to the next bush,
the bobber dips and back up.
One quick motion and nothing changes,
everything is gone.

CENTER CEMETERY, LONG BRANCH BAPTIST CHURCH

for Miss Allie Miles 1900-1984

There she sleeps
between the two, squared in by gray slate,
Luther T. on her right,
and W. Kay on her left.
They all come together at the head
reading MILES.
Spring, wild onions grow between
sand pebbles, rocks.
All over, centipede grass is spread flat,
planted by Luther some twenty years earlier,
his attempt to hold in loose dirt.
And here I am watching
as they try to keep the earth together,
a poor sand that grows
centipede, cactus, and the dead.

Just below my feet a killdeer
listens to footsteps.
She squawks and flaps,
racing around two of the stones,
and I forget for a moment why I am here.
I turn to walk toward her. Crying,
she darts at me and then away. I step
and her white wings fill out.

And then I remember Miss Allie
telling how the killdeer makes her nest
in a hole dug out of the ground.
Peering round I see a slough in the sand;
between two markers is her prize.
Gray, black speckled, the one egg
blends with the color of stone.
Turning away, and back to Miss Allie
I think how the living protect the unborn
and how the dead protect the living,
all of us holding our pieces together,
knowing the earth will rise
to claim us.

Even in the sun I feel the cold blow
and look over
at Granddaddy's place, at the dates,
and at the two or three beyond
that have only one date.

I close my eyes to the pine rows
at the back of the lot, the leaning
in my ears, the faint whimper
of the killdeer. Far away,
I barely hear the power saws
at Fort Creek Mill, cutting another pine
to fill a space, an empty date.

LATE THAT DAY

I cried for an hour till Miss Allie said she'd take me.
She gathered up the cane poles and I went behind the house
to dig some red wigglers from last year's horse dung.
Between my fingers I shoveled deep, dank muck of black,
reds, and gray-white jellies caked under my nails.
And again I thought of Sam in that stirred up water
like these worms crawling in darkness,
blindly led to the river to be washed clean.

Later, down at the sycamore fork,
a good four-mile walk from the head of the cove,
the water still and clear, lapped toward dusk.
We had been there about ten minutes
when we landed two largemouth and a catfish.
Around dark she hauled in a three pound crappie.
After that I caught nothing, cold.

POST HOLE DIGGING

And after the inside grew deep,
I took one end, she pulled the other,
hers swung high,
mine low
dragging most of the way.
She let me drop to the lip
of the hole and she hoisted skyward.
I grabbed the cedar
by its middle, hanging on
as if I had done it all along.
It rocked back and to, round
and round,
widening.
                Over one shoulder she heaved
the wooden handles
and paced her steps for the next one.
But I just kept swaying in circles,
my legs wrapped round,
holding on to all that was mine.
I closed my eyes,
my head spun
and again I rocked,
this time all the way to that angel blur.
Dizzy drunk, I dropped
and waited for the unwinding.

written in dingy white letters
on a green canopy tent flapping
hard against shadows. The water
runs off the top and puddles
halfway between each metal pole,
and the pallbearers move forward
with the box, only to come back
empty handed.

One just in front of me blocks my view.
The air is getting tight.
I step back, underneath one of the drips.
It hits me hard, deep in my hair
soaking the back of my collar
down my back catching my belt line.
I imagine the dark water,
green and white turning gray.

The preacher steps back,
the sermon over,
the earth taking back another aunt
along with the others, air tight,
in another one of those boxes.
Oh God, not me. Leave me
to the mulch and bog sand rot,
take me fire, Indian River Scotch-Irish
swamp water, my name is David Johnson.
My name is David Johnson. How plain.

I am four years old sitting in the bathroom
at Miss Allie's, staring at the floor,
my pants at my ankles.
My toes dangle just above the tile. I lean
forward to feel the cold porcelain.
Cold pain. I giggle and lean back.
I do it again and again.
I laugh till my belly aches breathless.

Give me the cold. The rocks deep on sandstone.
One more minute
with Miss Allie and then I'll let go,
those ancient Cherokee paintings,
deer, whitetail and mule leaping wildly
eating muscadines, elderberries and then running like mad
from boars into marsh thickets
to wait, to hunt, to eat,
to be eaten,
embalmed forever.

I am back in the rain.
They've dropped her deep,
the shovels in wet sand ring metal.
Tuning forks hitting notes for another dead song.
Maybe someday we'll get it right.

SOMEWHERE

The other night, 10:41 P.M.
everyone off in their rooms
doing what they do,
me alone longer
than those desperate cows
listening for the ring
of oak limb
against tin bucket.
In just over an hour
today will be gone.

I look across the living room
into the kitchen,
into a glass of ice water
sweating on the breakfast table.
Two small chunks
break loose from the rest,
float to the top
like rock diamonds,
figures
in the glass.
One, a distinct face,
you again,
your eyes burning warm.

Even in that cool water,
your eyes are bluer
than blue, Carolina blue, deep
blue, bluer than any sky.
You never speak
and neither does the other guy.
You've been gone
a long time,
yet somehow your eyes
say everything.
It's not that far.

I remember you at the radio,
in the faded brown armed chair,
the one with those brass brads.
No matter how loud
you could never hear.
Your callused hands shook
as you cranked the knob
to make it louder.
Sometimes I swore I would go deaf.

It's something how you never really hear some things.
It's something how you never really hear some things.

Tonight, I really think I see you say it again.
It's closer than you think,
a thin ribbon between here
and an everlasting eternity.

COUNTING

I

This is the old kitchen,
dried meat in red darkness, blending
in the stove light, orange light, going blue
in its center, residue of ground corn.
And in the corner, the deep freeze half empty.
It is late February, cold,
the sun just up,
thirty days till planting,
numbers in our head, a life long timeline.

We have counted, since the first day of frost,
to find the end of winter.
From across the field we watch Buckshot, a
beggar,
sometimes standing, or sometimes kneeling
outside my uncle's home,
asking for leftovers,
or for a minute on the phone.
He fingers those dark pennies
like they'll grow.
By now even the turnips have lost.
The cabbages, one by one, have given up
their heads, frozen leaves waiting
to be plowed under.

And somewhere, someone has told us
this is what we put back for
day in, and out, all summer.
It's the counting, something learned,
something we believe in.

II

Job with sores, Job in light,
outside the mansion, crouching
holding on. Satan on one side,
God on the other, who's tempting who?
The rich man's dogs
lick the marks.
The saliva, his body,
sounds of a healing song.
And when it was over
he was the better,
endurance pays the debtor.

III

And on the morning they find Buck
in a sand ditch, a gun to his side,
his son, Bird, takes to work for the first time.
The first day of summer, last day of school,
it is here, in the old kitchen we sit,
Miss Allie stirring.
It's not for us to ask why, someone tells.
He'll remember. He counts and keeps track,
doesn't He?
For when we rise
we'll understand better by and by.

I don't own this,
I'm a renter
of this space
this body.
I'm just taking it all in.
     Eyes, ears, nose,
lips, and tongue
twirling it into place.

Painting the inside
walls, alone
I'm kneeling under the humidity
in this steamy garden.
Picking, bean picking,
hot bean picking.
     Over the shoulder I toss them
into deep wicker
baskets.
The bugs are out
and it has rained for several days.
The red clay between my toes
eases me
into the ground
     its moist, red lips
wet, ready to take me back.
Mush under my nails.
The bees are holding quietly
buzzing back the pollen.

WRESTLING ALL NIGHT

In the dark we grappled all night,
my legs around your torso,
your clenched hands throwing weight
at my chest. Jacob and the devil,
who else could it be?

As kids, when we woke from one of those nights of not sleeping
you would say, *he wrestled the devil*
all night long. One leg up, I let go
and you took me spinning
round and round
an upheaval only the two of us could know.

And this morning I wake anxious, I can't get up, I'm immobile,
paralyzed. I lie and lose another job.
My hands no longer five years old,
your face no longer lean, smooth with middle age.
My hands are your face,
the look I can't get rid of,
the skin that sheds every season,
grows anew only to be the same.

From eight hundred miles away I see you,
here, that day in the diner
over pancakes and coffee,
your tired face weary of this place
that gives you nothing in return.
I see you now at home your face slow, weighted
and I hear your voice, maybe for the first time
you sound happy to see Christmas,
the new year coming on.
And somewhere deep
hands on hands, face to face, hands to face

you say, *it's all recorded somewhere you just can't see.*
And now, as many times as you told it, I forget
the story and the dream, what it was about, and even who won.

TWO WARM SPRING SUNDAYS

I

Yes without her we fell to our knees,
our small lively hands finally let down.
The scene is still, all of us milling about, grumbling,
waiting for the one to say, *we're ready.*
The moment seems timeless, almost constructed,
this holding cell conjured. The girls sit giggling,
playing with their hair. They are in fine white dresses.
The boys roam in circles, one or two trying to catch
a glimpse beyond the gauze window.
Aunt Sue and Grandma catch them
and send them to the center of the house.
The younger ones follow suit, echoing,
I won't peek. I won't peek.
Dallas, thirteen years old, the oldest of the children, says,
he doesn't need to see, *I have seen it all.*
We prance behind him and agree.

Two aunts stare at each other in amazement
and then burst into laughter. Sara on the settee,
and Lou in the recliner, both wonder out loud
who he heard that from.
His mother assures he didn't get it from her.

It all seems out of time, touch. But the words say it all.
This is spring, Easter, nineteen seventy something
and in through the door pops Uncle Ray,
his bad foot and all.
He hobbles in to tell us that the eggs are set,
one of which is plastic and full of money.
We all jump and grab our baskets, stampede for the door,
a family herd hurrying to find what the relatives have hidden,
all of us wanting to get the big prize.

II

A couple of years later, in Sunday School,
the teacher told us
to color what Easter meant to us.
Loftin, my younger cousin, drew that purple plastic egg.
When asked why, he said, it's *the one with the money.*
None of us were really sure.
I couldn't think of anything to draw.
      One girl was making a lily out of white and yellow chalk.
If ever I've loved anything it was this.
This moment, this girl holding on to her picture.
She too, dressed in white, her hair in pig tails.
Cross-eyed, she wore thick glasses
that made her eyes look twice the size.
      She took them off to draw.
I watched her all the way through. She seemed dazed
as if everything around her gone dark,
just color dust, paper,
and a blind lily moving from head to hand.

ONE FIELD OVER

In this late autumn afternoon,
I'll ask for nothing of the next moment.
None of this holding on. Shake loose
the sky while the water vapors rise
over Rock Creek, the moon
taking its due.

Across the field, the row of pines pulls the sun in
and down, and into the next
open one. The sky grows heavy and the clouds
are getting closer and closer
to the ground. It's all here.
This is what I've wanted
for so long.

I see the whole town walking from this field
downward, through the swamp bog path
into the opening. They are parading
with laughter, baskets of food, and jug ice tea.
They pull the tablecloth
over the open ground and spread dishes
over the four corners. The children toss
in the high grass, rolling the weeds back
and up
until they are covered.

Mama and Miss Allie butter the biscuits.
Daddy, Luther, uncles and Buckshot
tell stories. Granddaddy Russell stands to pray.
it begins to rain. Harder.
Still harder. The rhythm of prayer
falls over us, over Carolina,
the ground giving back its water,
moon water, and the darkness shuts us in.

MARBLE SHOOT

Well this is the sand that runs through stone,
the color that ripples through marbles
in the pocket, day old rocks I have won
at war, the circle of games drawn in the dirt.
     I would take them back now, but it's over.
I would air mail them, but it's done.
I would lay me down to sleep and forget the whole thing,
but the mind won't let us down when we most want.
     Outside this circle, I am a child, It's 1972,
before work, I'm on my knees
blowing warm luck over the Aggie Shooter,
praying not to lose another.
     I dream of Christmas, full
of fruit, nuts, candy, and a new bag of marbles.
Box them up and hold onto them, he would say.
Don't lose them all in one place.

And another Christmas, my sister sitting at the table,
wanting me to do something. The morning is heavy and
quiet,
the Frigidaire like a metronome is keeping time.
This is way too close, nothing is familiar.
     I am thinking of my mother, her eyes swollen
in morning. She is begging him to act that way in public.
He has walked out again dragging her behind,
a helpless need to help another.
     The grits are thickening and the coffee is past cold.
I have completely left my body.
Sister is crying. She wants to leave.
There is nowhere to go.

But this morning, twenty years later, Christmas,
dressed in my plow boots, I haven't *really* worked for years.
I am hiking up my pants
on his body. It's him in me.
    I have just realized I have nothing to say.
I never had and maybe . . .
Yes I am on my knees again this morning, begging for another win,
like he will be in another house.
    His wide smile and heavy laugh I beg
to hold me down, but it's Christmas,
the table is set and it's just the two of us.
My sister, myself.
    My face lightly reflects in the corner of the window.
And I know I am losing
every breath back, the whistle in his nose.
The giving of one body to another.

Father to mother to son to daughter,
giving one by one, and taking again.
Far away this morning I hear him reading
another story of father and son.
    And again my mind floats around the circle, the daylight draining.
No matter where you were you could shoot the marble,
the clicking, the sound of what we most want
and could never say.